Musings

E Kraft

BookLeaf Publishing

India | USA | UK

Presentation by *BookLeaf Publishing*

Web: www.bookleafpub.com

E-mail: info@bookleafpub.com

ISBN: 9789360942434

First edition 2024

Shadow to Adieu

I love you
Bawling all alone in rue
Feelings like a drunken stew
Fumbling pointlessly in the view
Of night, down the avenue
Cheap fluorescent lights' hue
Don't even give you a shadow to adieu

Simple Dazzle

The lovely chime rings upon entering
Mile-wide smiles envelope eager faces
Scanning the vast menu for the best one
"Sweet and bitter dancing in harmony"
As a new day rises
The melodious cafe comes to life
Out bursts freshly picked strawberries
Milk so frothy and overflowing
Matcha so smooth and lingering with umami
Topped with tapioca pearls so chewy and soft
"Had too matcha to drink?"
The day felt more dazzling than before!

Masked

Live like a rat
Not too much love, trust, anything
Don't cause offense
No arrogance, no peacocking

Raise your glasses to people you don't like
Add a dash of humor and small talk
Crack a sweet grin when they're looking
Suck up and sing praises: stupid empty words

Sickening, just sickening
The air is filled with angel's trumpets
A toxic red beauty
But pretend not to notice poison

Did I say too much?
Let me change that expression
Sorry, I'll act like your jester again
If I try hard enough,
Will you accept me?

Diversity

Amidst dark and drab sightings around
Sprinklings of rainbows still abound
Diversity flows into one luscious mound
As nature wakes the faded ground

Rainforests display beautiful sights
Plants and animals contribute their mites
One's uniqueness painting different lights
Making one reach ever greater heights

Many dull eyes shun brilliant rays
With their surprisingly unusual ways
But without them: how dark, dreary the days
But without them: how bleak, gloomy the bays

Each character with a role to fill
Each suit with a mosaic shield
We can jolt the world from its still
Spraying an endless kaleidoscopic field

Nature as our mentor sighs
Diversity as our brush flies
We can truly cloak this bland blank world
In buckets of paint fully swirled

Brownies

5

Each bite a melody of love
Flour and sugar in their own flirty waltz
Whisking up vibrant vanilla trances
Handcrafted just for glimpses of delights

So here with naked spatula in hand
Pour chocolate ambrosia straight from pious hearts

Car Crash

6

Streetlights cast long eerie shadows; sudden flash of
headlights
Whip past me then metal crushing, crumbling,
Angrily leaving careless trails of shattered glass,
The car wrap in a final losing wrestle against an ornery oak.

My heart pounds: a relentless drumbeat
Forever etched into the coarse fabric of my consciousness
Sirens wail lamentably moments later

The specter of mortality forever just beneath
Our seemingly ordinary lives.

Nourish

In the cave of human psyches
Echo shattered lives, shattered communities
Fraying the fabric of familial love
Young lives extinguished before they begun;
Suffocated by the web of pressures and despairs:
A chilling indictment of an indifferent world
Failing to protect its most vulnerable members

Justice taunts like a distant mirage
Silent shrieks of systemic injustices
Converging to breed a generation
Haunted by trauma, untreated mental illness
Where guns and knives replace words and empathy

Yet amidst the darkness flickers the faintest glimmer,
A collective resolve to heal the wounds,
To build a future where
Every life is cherished,
Every voice heard
Every dream nourished.

Alone

Alone
Once something to be feared
Searched frantically in the crowd
But your quick steps disappeared
I looked high above me
Still no familiar face
Just one gentle uniform
Escorting to the desk
The intercom yelled and yelled
You slowly re-appeared
A smirk on your face
Many times this act re-played

Alone
Now I am grown
Just freedom in the air
No more smirks to care

Complicated

Riding high, sharing secrets and laughs,
Then plummeting into a pit of drama and distrust
Never sure if the next step will solidify the bond
Or shatter it into irreparable pieces.
Yet a strange magnetic lure
Maybe the thrill of the unpredictable
Or the hope for genuine connection beneath it all.

Whatever it is, navigating the frenemy landscape
Teaches about loyalty, boundaries
And the complexities of relationships..

Roots

Soft tendrils transform to silver threads
Waltzing with the winds of time
Embracing life's jaunts and twists
Sly fingers stroking

Each strand a silent storyteller
Whispering of roots and resilience

Pruritus

Emerging suddenly, maddening
Creeping stealthily across the skin
First a gentle tickle, barely perceptible
Then insistent throbs commanding action,
Manifesting in inconvenient places,
Teasing unpredictably
Maybe a solitary annoyance or an army of prickling
sensations,
Then wildfire across the body, a relentless force that
demands relief.

The urge to scratch irresistible, a primal instinct overrides
rational thought
Yet, even as fingers delve into the skin
Temporary ecstasy of relief leads to more…itching
Reminder of the body's fragility and the complexities of
sensations.

Sugar Cane Dew

Sweet pungent dew
Flow long and clear
Run to the edge of pouting lips
A kiss to rescue the falling drop
Savor
Try to recapture its fleeting
Sugar-cane sweetness

Identity

In the sea of human consciousness,
Thoughts swirl into emotional eddies
Enigmatic waves of our existence
Splashes at the fringes of our perception
Blurring the ripples between reality and fantasy
Each heartbeat: a rebellion pulsing, pulsing against
artificial dams
Seeking the shadows' secrets

Finally in the silence of the night,
We confront the vastness of our uncertainty,
Tracing the contours of our identity
Far away in the stars.

Climb

perpetually up the hill: deadlines making the path ever
longer, endless struggle to balance class, activities, friends
and a desperate desire for a bit more time, me time.

elusive, insurmountable: why battle? who cares?

then an intermittent summit:
understand a complex concept, complete a particularly
protracted project,

a momentary deep breath overlooking the cliff,
making the ongoing climb worthwhile…   sometimes

Without Boundary

15

assaulted olfactorally by epic proportions:

my beloved canine companion once again:
a bouncing eau de wet dog with a hint of expired cheese,
aroma so pungent, so potent
even the hardiest of skunks run for cover.

how is it possible to produce such a cosmic stench?
foul fragrance that lingers in the air, refusing exorcism?

a constant reminder that true love knows no bounds,
not even the boundaries of good hygiene.

Lazy

Drawn to the sirens' calls of your iphone or anything that offers a momentary escape, constant battles between you and the shrewish voice reminding of the consequences of delaying, still despite the mounting anxiety and guilt, a strange comfort in the familiar, the cycle, the rush of adrenaline with last-minute scrambles, fueled by a combination of fear of failng and the ever-present belief in tomorrow to start anew.

A stubborn resistance to change, to break free from the frenemy's suffocating grip. The struggle is not just against time but against the very essence of human nature: the eternal battle between the comfort of the familiar and the uncertainty of the unknown!

Alas, better than just being lazy

Sharp Crusts

White fluff rises, a silent promise unfurls.
From humble grains and water's touch
Emerges bread naive and virginal
Crust crackles, whispers of comfort
Through laughter shared and secrets told

Sudden/ sharp crust slices
Stunned/ I watch redness pool on the tip of my finger
My tongue taste the metal twang of a friend's betrayal
In the echo of silence where trust once embraced
Crumbs of memories, now burnt remains

Humility hardens into inedible mound
Yet amidst the pain, a lesson learned
To find the strength to rise higher still.
To forgive one day though never forget
And build new bonds wherever God may lead:

New breads/friends can be delicious and true
But check for surprisingly sharp crusts!

Equity

Deeply entrenched in the fabric worldwide
Endless cycles of oppression and marginalization
Fueled by historical, systemic biases, power differentials

Injustices in myriad forms
Overt discrimination to subtle microaggressions
Re-shaping individuals' experiences
Undermining the fundamental principles of equality and
justice
Challenging the very essence of humanity:
Im-moral progress and collective conscience-less

Yet the three musketeers of education, empathy, reform
Can dismantle, can heal
For inclusive societies
For equitability and harmony for all.

Ode to Black Holes

19

My dear black holes,
Mysterious creatures from large stars
Nuclear fusions from crushing hydrogens into heliums
Delicately balancing between radiation and gravity

Until their supernova explosion
Just a fraction of a second
Pity no one can see

My dear black holes
Though misconstrued like dull vacuums
A new generation will look to you
And will one day uncover the real you

The Baker

I used to be a baker
But couldn't handle the heat,
Couldn't rise to the occasion
After kneading dough.

So I was a tailor
But soon lost my thread;
I made belts from watches
But all were waists of time.

So then I tried banking
But overdrew and bounced,
Frankly lost my interest
Couldn't make more cents.

So here I am, a kid again
Gladly off to school
Though my math has problems,
My pencil draws 'tention still.

Possibilities

Beyond letters, beyond words
Inscribe the depths of sentiments,
Both a refuge and a reckoning in the face of despair:
Navigate the labyrinthine corridors of disillusionment,
Seek solace in the silent echoes of verse.

For in the cadence of poetry lies power
To validate, to mend the wounded
Amidst shadows of defeat: glimpse beauty, hope,
redemption
Amidst shattered dreams: a voice, a sanctuary, a
community

Explore the depths of humanity, confront unknown demons
Embrace the possibility of renewal and transformation.
For in the fragile interplay of ink and emotion,
Lies the promise of redemption, the legacy of resilience

Poetry wraps the complexities of existence
In a blanket of sanguine possibilities.

www.ingramcontent.com/pod-product-compliance
Lightning Source LLC
Chambersburg PA
CBHW071257140726
47996CB00007B/2875